Copyright © 2019, 2014, 2011, 2009 WINGS Curriculum, LLC. All Rights Reserved.

All of the logos, artwork, designs, and activities in this publication are exclusively owned by WINGS Curriculum, LLC and are protected under copyright law. Unauthorized reproduction is prohibited.

Written by Dr. Bisa Batten Lewis.
Book design, logos, artwork, and illustrations by Phillip L. Harper, Jr.
Cover design by Kumar V

REPRODUCTION RIGHTS

Permission is granted to individual teachers to reproduce copies of forms - only in the *WINGS Curriculum Book of Forms* and accompanying electronic forms and e-books for the specific use of his/her individual classroom.

Reproducing materials outside the scope of these rights is a violation of copyright laws. All menus, materials, PDF's and other materials contained in the WINGS Curriculum are the sole the property of WINGS Curriculum, LLC. Any reproduction, misuse, or using these products for profitable gain is unlawful and is strictly forbidden. Legal action will be taken against any violators of these rights.

Table of Contents

I. Assessing & Evaluating Progress 2
    A. Anecdotal Record Form.. 2
    B. Individual Child Portfolio Checklist.. 3
    C. Classroom Transition Letter... 4
    D. Individualized Assessment Form... 5
    E. Class/Group Assessment Form.. 6
    F. Progress Report for Infants 7
    G. Progress Report for Toddlers: 1 Year–Olds 9
    H. Progress Report for Toddlers: 2 Year–Olds 11
    I. Progress Report for Preschoolers: 3 Year–Olds 13
    J. Progress Report for Preschoolers: 4 & 5 Year–Olds.. 15
    K. Data Collection Forms 17

II. Planning Daily Activities 42
    A. My Ideal Daily Activity Schedule 42
    B. Daily Activity Form for Infants/1 Year-Olds 43
    C. Developmental Activity Plan for Infants... 44
    D. Weekly Lesson Plans for Infants... 45
    E. Weekly Lesson Plans for Toddlers 46
    F. Weekly Lesson Plans for Preschoolers/Pre-K.. 49
    G. Weekly Lesson Plans for Blended Classrooms... 52
    H. Weekly Lesson Plans for Family/Group Day Care 55
    I. Weekly Lesson Plans for Extended Day/After-School: Infants 58
    J. Weekly Lesson Plans for Extended Day/After-School: Toddlers 59
    K. Weekly Lesson Plans for Extended Day/After-School: Preschoolers/Pre-K............... 60

III. Record-Keeping Forms 61
    A. Health Check Form.. 61
    B. Student Incident Report Form 62
    C. All About My Day/Week Forms... 63
    D. Parent Orientation Checklist 64
    E. Parent Conference Form 65
    F. Parent Conference Evaluation 66
    G. Home Connections Form.. 67

Anecdotal Record

Child's Name Age Y M

Observer Date

Setting Time

Incident

Interpretation

Developmental Area(s) ☐ P ☐ SE ☐ LL ☐ AL ☐ C

Anecdotal Record

Child's Name Age Y M

Observer Date

Setting Time

Incident

Interpretation

Developmental Area(s) ☐ P ☐ SE ☐ LL ☐ AL ☐ C

Anecdotal Record

Child's Name Age Y M

Observer Date

Setting Time

Incident

Interpretation

Developmental Area(s) ☐ P ☐ SE ☐ LL ☐ AL ☐ C

Anecdotal Record

Child's Name Age Y M

Observer Date

Setting Time

Incident

Interpretation

Developmental Area(s) ☐ P ☐ SE ☐ LL ☐ AL ☐ C

WINGS Individual Child Portfolio Checklist

Child's Name _____ **Date Enrolled** _____

A complete *WINGS Individual Child Portfolio* includes:

- ☐ *WINGS Anecdotal Records* (Teacher observations)
- ☐ *WINGS Individualized Assessments*
- ☐ *WINGS Progress Reports*
- ☐ A collection of work samples showing advancement, regression, or consistent achievement over time:
  - Dated series of child's artwork and/or writing
  - Log of favorite books, songs, and finger plays
  - Photos of child demonstrating skills or engaging in activities
  - Audio or video of child speaking, singing, storytelling, etc.
  - Parent Conferences/Interviews/Reports and/or Questionnaires
- ☐ Annual photo of the child
- ☐ Other important documents

Transition & Tracking

Date _____ Classroom _____ Teacher's Name _____

Date _____ Classroom _____ Teacher's Name _____

Date _____ Classroom _____ Teacher's Name _____

Date _____ Classroom _____ Teacher's Name _____

Date _____ Classroom _____ Teacher's Name _____

Date _____ Classroom _____ Teacher's Name _____

Date _____ Classroom _____ Teacher's Name _____

Date _____ Classroom _____ Teacher's Name _____

For purposes of confidentiality, it is not recommended that the portfolio be shared with teachers outside of the program. Sharing the portfolio is the parent's rightful choice.

WINGS Classroom Transition Letter

Date _____

Dear _____ :

_____ has made progress in _____ . Because of
    [Child's Name]   **[Current Classroom]**

progress and age, it is now time for your child to begin transition to _____ .
                                                                               [New Classroom]

_____ will transition according to the following schedule:
   [Child's Name]

Infants and Toddlers

Week 1: _____ through _____ 9:00 a.m.–10:00 a.m.

Week 2: _____ through _____ 9:00 a.m.–11:00 a.m.

Week 3: _____ through _____ 9:00 a.m.–12:00 p.m.

Week 4: _____ through _____ 8:00 a.m.–3:00 p.m.

Preschoolers

Week 1: _____ through _____ 9:00 a.m.–12:00 p.m.

Week 2: _____ through _____ 8:00 a.m.–3:00 p.m.

Effective, _____ your child will be added to the full-time roster of
         [Date of Full Transition]

_____ . _____ will be your child's new
  [New Classroom]   **[New Teacher]**

teacher.

Tuition will: ❏ Change to _____

             ❏ Remain the same.

If you have any questions, please feel free to contact me at _____ .

Sincerely,

cc: New Classroom Teacher
    Center Director

WINGS Individualized Assessment Form

Instructions: Record the WINGS of each child. This information will allow you to appropriately plan for individuals.

Child's Name _____ **Age** _____ Y _____ M

Wonder	**I**nterests	**N**eeds	**G**oals	**S**kills
			Cognitive:	*Cognitive:*
			Physical:	*Physical:*
			Social/Emotional:	*Social/Emotional:*
			Approaches to Learning:	*Approaches to Learning:*
			Language/Literacy:	*Language/Literacy:*

Date Completed _____ **Teacher(s)** _____

WINGS Class/Group Assessment Form

Instructions: Summarize your findings by recording all the WINGS you documented during individual assessments. This information will allow you to appropriately plan for changes in the environment and activities. You may find the need to group children according to their WINGS during specific small group activities. Record the Class/Group Assessment data on WINGS Sticky Notes, then post on the WINGS Wall.

Class/Group _____

Wonder	**I**nterests	**N**eeds	**G**oals	**S**kills
			Cognitive: *Physical:* *Social/Emotional:* *Approaches to Learning:* *Language/Literacy:*	*Cognitive:* *Physical:* *Social/Emotional:* *Approaches to Learning:* *Language/Literacy:*

Date Completed _____ **Teacher(s)** _____

WINGS Progress Report for Infants

Child's Name _____ Age ___ Y ___ M

Checkpoint: ☐ Fall ☐ Winter ☐ Spring ☐ Summer

Stages of Progress: − =Regressing + =Making Advancements ✓ =Shows Consistent Achievement

Physical	Social–Emotional	Language & Literacy	Approaches to Learning	Cognitive
☐ P1. Demonstrates awareness and control of head and body	☐ SE1. Demonstrates attachment toward adults	☐ LL1. Responds to commonsounds	☐ AL1. Begins to show interest and eagerness in exploring the environment	**Math** ☐ C-M1. Uses senses to examine objects of different shapes, sizes, features
☐ P2. Demonstrates beginning coordination	☐ SE2. Reacts differently toward familiar and unfamiliar adults	☐ LL2. Responds to frequently spoken words	☐ AL2. Repeats actions	**Science** ☐ C-SI1. Experiments with objects to see how they work
☐ P3. Demonstrates balance with support	☐ SE3. Demonstrates awareness of peers	☐ LL3. Follows simple directions and requests	☐ AL3. Uses gestures and motions to describe thoughts and actions	☐ C-SI3. Examines and explores the environment
☐ P4. Demonstrates control of hands and fingers	☐ SE4. Demonstrates awareness of peers' feelings	☐ LL4. Begins to use motions and gestures to communicate	☐ AL4. Uses sounds to describe thoughts and actions	**Social Studies** ☐ C-SS1. Recognizes significant family relationships
☐ P5. Begins to coordinate motions using eyes and hands	☐ SE5. Begins to develop self-awareness	☐ LL5. Uses sounds to communicate		☐ C-SS2. Demonstrates beginning awareness of cause and effect
☐ P6. Begins to help with feeding	☐ SE6. Demonstrates beginning awareness of own abilities	☐ LL6. Uses sounds in social situations		**Processes of Thought** ☐ C-TP1. Begins to demonstrate problem solving skills
☐ P7. Begins to help with dressing		☐ LL7. Begins to express self freely and creatively using sounds		**Creative Development** ☐ C-CD1. Begins to use voice, body, instruments, and objects to express creativity
☐ P8. Begins to help with routine health and personal hygiene practices		☐ LL8. Attends to stories		
☐ P9. Responds to verbal/physical danger signals		☐ LL9. Explores books		
☐ P10. Uses senses to explore environment		☐ LL10. Demonstrates awareness of pictures		

Date Completed _____ Teacher(s) _____

Supporting Evidence/Data	
❏ WINGS Anecdotal Records Dates: _____ _____ _____	❏ WINGS Individualized Assessment Dates: _____ _____ _____
❏ WINGS Individual Child Portfolio Artifacts Dates: _____ _____ _____	❏ Other Dates: _____ _____ _____

Teacher Comments: _____

_____

_____

_____

Concerns: _____

_____

_____

_____

Next Steps: _____

_____

_____

_____

Date Completed _____ **Completed By** _____

Shared with Parent(s)/Guardian(s) on _____

Parent(s)/Guardian(s) Signature _____

WiNGS Progress Report for Toddlers: 1 Year–Olds

Child's Name _____ Age ___ Y ___ M

Checkpoint: ☐ Fall ☐ Winter ☐ Spring ☐ Summer

Stages of Progress: **−** =Regressing **+** =Making Advancements **✓** =Shows Consistent Achievement

Physical	Social–Emotional	Language & Literacy	Approaches to Learning	Cognitive
☐ P2. Demonstrates beginning coordination	☐ SE4. Demonstrates awareness of peers' feelings	☐ LL3. Follows simple directions and requests	☐ AL5. Begins to show curiosity in the environment	**Math**
☐ P6. Begins to help with feeding	☐ SE7. Demonstrates feelings of security and trust with familiar adults	☐ LL5. Uses sounds to communicate	☐ AL6. Begins to find different ways to solve different problems	☐ C-M1. Uses senses to examine objects of different shapes, sizes, features
☐ P7. Begins to help with dressing	☐ SE8. Builds relationships with adults	☐ LL6. Uses sounds in social situations	☐ AL7. Begins to focus on activities of interest	☐ C-M2. Begins to sort and match with assistance
☐ P8. Begins to help with routine health and personal hygiene practices	☐ SE9. Begins to build relationships with other children	☐ LL11. Responds to spoken words	☐ AL8. Begins to show persistence in learning and discovery	**Science Inquiry**
☐ P9. Responds to verbal/physical danger signals	☐ SE10. Demonstrates sense of self-preferences and differences	☐ LL12. Communicates non-verbally	☐ AL9. Begins to use words to describe thoughts and actions	☐ C-SI1. Experiments with objects to see how they work
☐ P10. Uses senses to explore environment	☐ SE11. Demonstrates awareness of own abilities	☐ LL13. Begins to communicate orally using sounds and words		☐ C-SI2. Examines and explores the environment
☐ P11. Controls movements of arms and legs	☐ SE12. Regulates emotions and behaviors with support	☐ LL14. Begins to express self freely and creatively using sounds and words		**Social Studies**
☐ P12. Demonstrates balance without support		☐ LL15. Asks simple questions		☐ C-SS1. Recognizes significant family relationships
☐ P13. Coordinates motions using hands and fingers		☐ LL16. Listens to short stories		☐ C-SS2. Demonstrates beginning awareness of cause and effect
☐ P14. Demonstrates eye-hand coordination		☐ LL17. Explores book features with hands and fingers		**Processes of Thought**
☐ P15. Begins to help with routine tasks		☐ LL18. Demonstrates awareness of pictures within print		☐ C-TP1. Begins to demonstrate problem solving skills
☐ P16. Demonstrate beginning awareness of personal health needs		☐ LL19. Scribbles spontaneously		**Creative Development**
				☐ C-CD2. Begins to express creativity through musical use of voice, instruments, and objects
				☐ C-CD3. Begins to express creativity through dance
				☐ C-CD4. Begins to express creativity through drama
				☐ C-CD5. Begins to express creativity through visual art forms

Date Completed _____ Teacher(s) _____

Supporting Evidence/Data	
❏ WINGS Anecdotal Records Dates: _____ _____ _____	❏ WINGS Individualized Assessment Dates: _____ _____ _____
❏ WINGS Individual Child Portfolio Artifacts Dates: _____ _____ _____	❏ Other Dates: _____ _____ _____

Teacher Comments: _____

_____

_____

_____

Concerns: _____

_____

_____

_____

Next Steps: _____

_____

_____

_____

Date Completed _____ **Completed By** _____

Shared with Parent(s)/Guardian(s) on _____

Parent(s)/Guardian(s) Signature _____

WINGS Progress Report for Toddlers: 2 Year-Olds

Child's Name _____ Age ___ Y ___ M

Checkpoint: ☐ Fall ☐ Winter ☐ Spring ☐ Summer

Stages of Progress: **−** =Regressing **+** =Making Advancements **✓** =Shows Consistent Achievement

Physical	Social–Emotional	Language & Literacy	Approaches to Learning	Cognitive	

Physical	Social–Emotional	Language & Literacy	Approaches to Learning	Cognitive
☐ P11. Controls movements of arms and legs	☐ SE12. Regulates emotions and behaviors with support	☐ LL11. Responds to spoken words	☐ AL10. Shows curiosity in the environment	**Math**
☐ P12. Demonstrates balance without support	☐ SE13. Demonstrates feelings of security and trust	☐ LL12. Communicates non-verbally	☐ AL11. Finds new solutions to problems	☐ C-M1. Uses senses to examine objects of different shapes, sizes, features
☐ P13. Coordinates motions using hands and fingers	☐ SE14. Seeks to build relationships and social skills with adults	☐ LL20. Follows two-step directions and requests	☐ AL12. Focuses on activities of interest	☐ C-M2. Begins to sort and match with assistance
☐ P14. Demonstrates eye-hand coordination	☐ SE15. Begins to develop relationships and social skills with peers	☐ LL21. Uses words in social situations	☐ AL13. Shows persistence in learning and discovery	☐ C-M3. Demonstrates awareness of quantity and number concepts
☐ P17. Demonstrates coordination	☐ SE16. Demonstrates sensitivity toward feelings of peers	☐ LL22. Begins to communicate orally using words	☐ AL14. Uses words to describe thoughts and actions	☐ C-M4. Begins to identify basic shapes
☐ P18. Feeds self	☐ SE17. Demonstrates knowledge of self-preferences and differences	☐ LL23. Expresses self creatively using words		☐ C-M5. Demonstrates beginning awareness of measurement concepts
☐ P19. Helps dress self	☐ SE18. Demonstrates confidence in abilities	☐ LL24. Asks questions		☐ C-M6. Explores patterns
☐ P20. Helps with routine health and personal hygiene practices		☐ LL25. Follows what happens in a story		☐ C-M7. Demonstrates mathematical thinking in problem solving
☐ P21. Pays attention to safety instructions		☐ LL26. Explores book features with beginning awareness		**Science Inquiry**
☐ P22. Uses senses to explore environment and process information		☐ LL27. Demonstrates awareness of pictures and symbols within print		☐ C-SI3. Uses simple tools to experiment
☐ P23. Helps with routine tasks		☐ LL28. Begins to differentiate between sounds in language		☐ C-SI4. Explores geographical concepts
☐ P24. Demonstrates awareness of personal health needs		☐ LL29. Scribbles to imitate and explore		
☐ P25. Participates in activities related to nutrition		☐ LL30. Draws pictures		
☐ P26. Coordinates body movements in relation to objects and space				

Social Studies
- ☐ C-SS3. Recognizes family roles
- ☐ C-SS4. Recognizes community roles

Processes of Thought
- ☐ C-TP2. Demonstrates logical reasoning in problem solving
- ☐ C-TP3. Demonstrates awareness of cause and effect

Creative Development
- ☐ C-CD2. Begins to express creativity through musical use of voice, instruments, and objects
- ☐ C-CD3. Begins to express creativity through dance
- ☐ C-CD4. Begins to express creativity through drama
- ☐ C-CD5. Begins to express creativity through visual art forms

Date Completed _____ Teacher(s) _____

11

Supporting Evidence/Data

❏ WINGS Anecdotal Records	❏ WINGS Individualized Assessment
Dates: _____ _____ _____	Dates: _____ _____ _____
❏ WINGS Individual Child Portfolio Artifacts	❏ Other
Dates: _____ _____ _____	Dates: _____ _____ _____

Teacher Comments: _____

_____

_____

_____

Concerns: _____

_____

_____

_____

Next Steps: _____

_____

_____

_____

Date Completed _____   **Completed By** _____

Shared with Parent(s)/Guardian(s) on _____

Parent(s)/Guardian(s) Signature _____

WINGS Progress Report for Preschoolers: 3 Year–Olds

Child's Name _____   Age ___ Y ___ M

Checkpoint: ☐ Fall ☐ Winter ☐ Spring ☐ Summer

Stages of Progress: − =Regressing   + =Making Advancements   ✓ =Shows Consistent Achievement

Physical	Social-Emotional	Language & Literacy	Approaches to Learning	Cognitive	
☐ P12. Demonstrates balance without support	☐ SE13. Demonstrates feelings of security and trust	☐ LL11. Responds to spoken words	☐ AL14. Uses words to describe thoughts and actions	**Math**	**Social Studies**
☐ P13. Coordinates motions using hands and fingers	☐ SE16. Demonstrates sensitivity toward feelings of peers	☐ LL12. Communicates nonverbally	☐ AL15. Shows persistence in activities of interest	☐ C-M3. Demonstrates awareness of quantity and number concepts	☐ C-SS5. Demonstrates understanding of family and emerging awareness of culture
☐ P14. Demonstrates eye-hand coordination	☐ SE17. Demonstrates knowledge of self-preferences and differences	☐ LL21. Uses words in social situations	☐ AL16. Shows curiosity in learning new things	☐ C-M6. Explores patterns	☐ C-SS6. Demonstrates understanding of community and emerging awareness of others' cultures
☐ P17. Demonstrates coordination	☐ SE18. Demonstrates confidence in abilities	☐ LL23. Expresses self creatively using words	☐ AL17. Begins to show persistence in assorted tasks	☐ C-M7. Demonstrates mathematical thinking in problem solving	☐ C-SS7. Explores geographical concepts related to local community
☐ P18. Feeds self	☐ SE19. Regulates emotions and behaviors regularly	☐ LL24. Asks questions	☐ AL18. Finds creative solutions to problems	☐ C-M8. Sorts and matches	**Processes of Thought**
☐ P21. Pays attention to safety instructions	☐ SE20. Develops relationships and social skills with adults	☐ LL29. Scribbles to imitate and explore		☐ C-M9. Explores, recognizes and describes basic shapes and shape concepts	☐ C-TP2. Demonstrates logical reasoning in problem solving
☐ P22. Uses senses to explore environment and process information	☐ SE21. Develops relationships and social skills with peers	☐ LL30. Draws pictures		☐ C-M10. Demonstrates awareness of measurement concepts	☐ C-TP3. Demonstrates awareness of cause and effect
☐ P23. Helps with routine tasks	☐ SE22. Uses adults as a resource	☐ LL31. Follows three-step directions and requests		☐ C-M11. Explores spatial concepts	☐ C-TP4. Uses prior knowledge to build new knowledge
☐ P24. Demonstrates awareness of personal health needs	☐ SE23. Develops friendships with peers	☐ LL32. Communicates orally using words		**Science Inquiry**	**Creative Development**
☐ P25. Participates in activities related to nutrition		☐ LL33. Demonstrates story logic		☐ C-SI5. Intentionally uses tools to experiment and explore	☐ C-CD6. Expresses creativity through musical use of voice, instruments, and objects
☐ P26. Coordinates body movements in relation to objects and space		☐ LL34. Demonstrates awareness of book features		☐ C-SI6. Explores concepts related to life science	☐ C-CD7. Expresses creativity through dance
☐ P27. Dresses self		☐ LL35. Develops knowledge of print		☐ C-SI7. Explores concepts related to earth science	☐ C-CD8. Expresses creativity through drama
☐ P28. Attends to routine health and personal hygiene practices		☐ LL36. Differentiates sounds of language		☐ C-SI8. Explores concepts related to physical science	☐ C-CD9. Expresses creativity through visual art forms
☐ P29. Identifies healthy food choices		☐ LL37. Creatively expresses using writing skills			
		☐ LL38. Demonstrates beginning knowledge of the alphabet			

Date Completed _____   Teacher(s) _____

Supporting Evidence/Data

☐ **WINGS Anecdotal Records**

Dates:
_____
_____
_____

☐ **WINGS Individualized Assessment**

Dates:
_____
_____
_____

☐ **WINGS Individual Child Portfolio Artifacts**

Dates:
_____
_____
_____

☐ **Other**

Dates:
_____
_____
_____

Teacher Comments: _____

_____

_____

_____

Concerns: _____

_____

_____

_____

Next Steps: _____

_____

_____

_____

Date Completed _____ **Completed By** _____

Shared with Parent(s)/Guardian(s) on _____

Parent(s)/Guardian(s) Signature _____

WINGS Progress Report for Preschoolers: 4 & 5 Year-Olds

Child's Name _____ Age ___ Y ___ M

Checkpoint: ☐ Fall ☐ Winter ☐ Spring ☐ Summer

Stages of Progress: – = Regressing   + = Making Advancements   ✓ = Shows Consistent Achievement

Physical	Social–Emotional	Language & Literacy	Approaches to Learning	Cognitive
☐ P12. Demonstrates balance without support	☐ SE13. Demonstrates feelings of security and trust	☐ LL11. Responds to spoken words	☐ AL16. Shows curiosity in learning new things	**Math**
☐ P13. Coordinates motions using hands and fingers	☐ SE16. Demonstrates sensitivity toward feelings of peers	☐ LL12. Communicates non-verbally	☐ AL18. Finds creative solutions to problems	☐ C-M9. Explores, recognizes and describes basic shapes and shape concepts
☐ P14. Demonstrates eye-hand coordination	☐ SE17. Demonstrates knowledge of self-preferences and differences	☐ LL21. Uses words in social situations	☐ AL19. Shows persistence in assorted tasks	☐ C-M12. Develops knowledge, representation, comparison and manipulation of quantity and number concepts
☐ P17. Demonstrates coordination	☐ SE18. Demonstrates confidence in abilities	☐ LL23. Expresses self creatively using words	☐ AL20. Begins and completes activities with persistence and attention	☐ C-M13. Uses mathematical thinking, reasoning, problem solving, and estimation
☐ P18. Feeds self	☐ SE19. Regulates emotions and behaviors regularly	☐ LL32. Communicates orally using words	☐ AL21. Shows interest in engaging in group activities	☐ C-M14. Sorts, classifies, seriates, and creates patterns
☐ P21. Pays attention to safety instructions	☐ SE20. Develops relationships and social skills with adults	☐ LL33. Demonstrates story logic	☐ AL22. Shows independence in learning	☐ C-M15. Explores and communicates measurement concepts – time, weight, distance, length, height
☐ P22. Uses senses to explore environment and process information	☐ SE21. Develops relationships and social skills with peers	☐ LL35. Develops knowledge of print		☐ C-M16. Explores, recognizes and describes spatial relationships
☐ P23. Helps with routine tasks	☐ SE22. Uses adults as a resource	☐ LL36. Differentiates sounds of language		**Science Inquiry**
☐ P24. Demonstrates awareness of personal health needs	☐ SE23. Develops friendships with peers	☐ LL39. Follows three(+)-step directions and requests		☐ C-SI5. Intentionally uses tools to experiment and explore
☐ P25. Participates in activities related to nutrition		☐ LL40. Demonstrates increasing knowledge of the alphabet		☐ C-SI9. Demonstrates knowledge of life science
☐ P26. Coordinates body movements in relation to objects and space		☐ LL41. Develops knowledge of book features		☐ C-SI10. Demonstrates knowledge of earth science
☐ P27. Dresses self		☐ LL42. Listens to comprehend		☐ C-SI11. Demonstrates knowledge of physical science
☐ P28. Attends to routine health and personal hygiene practices		☐ LL43. Demonstrates understanding of new vocabulary in conversations, stories/books, and activities		☐ C-SI12. Uses scientific processes to actively explore and increase understanding of environment
☐ P29. Identifies healthy food choices		☐ LL44. Exhibits 2,000-word vocabulary		**Social Studies**
☐ P30. Demonstrates strength		☐ LL45. Asks detailed questions		☐ C-SS5. Demonstrates understanding of family and emerging awareness of culture
☐ P31. Identifies healthy and safe living practices		☐ LL46. Creatively expresses through writing skills and drawing		☐ C-SS6. Demonstrates understanding of community and emerging awareness of others' cultures
		☐ LL47. Develops writing abilities		☐ C-SS8. Demonstrates consideration for individual differences
		☐ LL48. Develops early phonological awareness		☐ C-SS9. Demonstrates awareness of demographics and economy of local community
				☐ C-SS10. Demonstrates awareness of historical events and relevance to current events
				Processes of Thought
				☐ C-TP2. Demonstrates logical reasoning in problem solving
				☐ C-TP3. Demonstrates awareness of cause and effect
				☐ C-TP4. Uses prior knowledge to build new knowledge
				Creative Development
				☐ C-CD6. Expresses creativity through musical use of voice, instruments, and objects
				☐ C-CD7. Expresses creativity through dance
				☐ C-CD8. Expresses creativity through drama
				☐ C-CD9. Expresses creativity through visual art forms

Date Completed _____ Teacher(s) _____

Supporting Evidence/Data	
☐ WINGS Anecdotal Records Dates: _____ _____ _____	☐ WINGS Individualized Assessment Dates: _____ _____ _____
☐ WINGS Individual Child Portfolio Artifacts Dates: _____ _____ _____	☐ Other Dates: _____ _____ _____

Teacher Comments: _____

_____

_____

_____

Concerns: _____

_____

_____

_____

Next Steps: _____

_____

_____

_____

Date Completed _____   **Completed By** _____

Shared with Parent(s)/Guardian(s) on _____

Parent(s)/Guardian(s) Signature _____

Classroom Data Collection for Infants
PHYSICAL DEVELOPMENT

Teacher _____ Classroom _____ Date _____

Stages of Progress: — =*Regressing* **+** =*Making Advancements* ✓ =*Shows Consistent Achievement*

Child's Name	Physical Development										Notes
	P1	P2	P3	P4	P5	P6	P7	P8	P9	P10	
1.											
2.											
3.											
4.											
5.											
6.											
7.											
8.											
9.											
10.											
11.											
12.											
13.											
14.											
15.											
16.											
17.											
18.											
19.											
20.											

WINGS Classroom Data Collection for Infants
SOCIAL/EMOTIONAL

Teacher _____ Classroom _____ Date _____

Stages of Progress: **−** =Regressing **+** =Making Advancements **✓** =Shows Consistent Achievement

Child's Name	Social/Emotional						Notes
	SE1	SE2	SE3	SE4	SE5	SE6	
1.							
2.							
3.							
4.							
5.							
6.							
7.							
8.							
9.							
10.							
11.							
12.							
13.							
14.							
15.							
16.							
17.							
18.							
19.							
20.							

WINGS
Classroom Data Collection for Infants
LANGUAGE & LITERACY

Teacher _____ Classroom _____ Date _____

Stages of Progress: **−** =Regressing **+** =Making Advancements **✓** =Shows Consistent Achievement

Child's Name	Language & Literacy										Notes
	LL1	LL2	LL3	LL4	LL5	LL6	LL7	LL8	LL9	LL10	
1.											
2.											
3.											
4.											
5.											
6.											
7.											
8.											
9.											
10.											
11.											
12.											
13.											
14.											
15.											
16.											
17.											
18.											
19.											
20.											

WINGS Classroom Data Collection for Infants
APPROACHES TO LEARNING

Teacher _____ Classroom _____ Date _____

Stages of Progress: **−** =Regressing **+** =Making Advancements **✓** =Shows Consistent Achievement

Child's Name	Cognitive				Notes
	AL1	AL2	AL3	AL4	
1.					
2.					
3.					
4.					
5.					
6.					
7.					
8.					
9.					
10.					
11.					
12.					
13.					
14.					
15.					
16.					
17.					
18.					
19.					
20.					

Classroom Data Collection for Infants
COGNITIVE

Teacher_____ Classroom_____ Date_____

Stages of Progress: −=*Regressing* +=*Making Advancements* ✓=*Shows Consistent Achievement*

Child's Name	Cognitive							Notes
	C-M1	C-SI1	C-SI2	C-SS1	C-SS2	C-TP1	C-CD1	
1.								
2.								
3.								
4.								
5.								
6.								
7.								
8.								
9.								
10.								
11.								
12.								
13.								
14.								
15.								
16.								
17.								
18.								
19.								
20.								

WiNGS Classroom Data Collection for Toddlers: 1 Year-Olds
PHYSICAL DEVELOPMENT

Teacher _____ Classroom _____ Date _____

Stages of Progress: **−** =Regressing   **+** =Making Advancements   **✓** =Shows Consistent Achievement

Child's Name	Physical Development															Notes
	P2	P6	P7	P8	P9	P10	P11	P12	P13	P14	P15	P16				
1.																
2.																
3.																
4.																
5.																
6.																
7.																
8.																
9.																
10.																
11.																
12.																
13.																
14.																
15.																
16.																
17.																
18.																
19.																
20.																

WINGS
Classroom Data Collection for Toddlers: 1 Year-Olds
SOCIAL/EMOTIONAL

Teacher _____ Classroom _____ Date _____

Stages of Progress: — =Regressing **+** =Making Advancements ✓ =Shows Consistent Achievement

Child's Name	Social/Emotional									Notes
	SE4	SE7	SE8	SE9	SE10	SE11	SE12			
1.										
2.										
3.										
4.										
5.										
6.										
7.										
8.										
9.										
10.										
11.										
12.										
13.										
14.										
15.										
16.										
17.										
18.										
19.										
20.										

Classroom Data Collection for Toddlers: 1 Year-Olds
LANGUAGE & LITERACY

Teacher _____ Classroom _____ Date _____

Stages of Progress: −=Regressing +=Making Advancements ✓=Shows Consistent Achievement

Child's Name	Language & Literacy													Notes
	LL3	LL5	LL6	LL11	LL12	LL13	LL14	LL15	LL16	LL17	LL18	LL19		
1.														
2.														
3.														
4.														
5.														
6.														
7.														
8.														
9.														
10.														
11.														
12.														
13.														
14.														
15.														
16.														
17.														
18.														
19.														
20.														

Classroom Data Collection for Toddlers: 1 Year-Olds
APPROACHES TO LEARNING

Teacher _____ Classroom _____ Date _____

Stages of Progress: — =*Regressing* ✚ =*Making Advancements* ✓ =*Shows Consistent Achievement*

Child's Name	Cognitive					Notes
	AL5	AL6	AL7	AL8	AL9	
1.						
2.						
3.						
4.						
5.						
6.						
7.						
8.						
9.						
10.						
11.						
12.						
13.						
14.						
15.						
16.						
17.						
18.						
19.						
20.						

WiNGS Classroom Data Collection for Toddlers: 1 Year-Olds
COGNITIVE

Teacher _____ Classroom _____ Date _____

Stages of Progress: — = *Regressing*   + = *Making Advancements*   ✓ = *Shows Consistent Achievement*

Child's Name	Cognitive										Notes
	C-M1	C-M2	C-SI1	C-SI2	C-SS1	C-SS2	C-TP1	C-CD2	C-CD3	C-CD4	C-CD5
1.											
2.											
3.											
4.											
5.											
6.											
7.											
8.											
9.											
10.											
11.											
12.											
13.											
14.											
15.											
16.											
17.											
18.											
19.											
20.											

Classroom Data Collection for Toddlers: 2 Year-Olds
PHYSICAL DEVELOPMENT

Teacher _____ Classroom _____ Date _____

Stages of Progress: **—** =Regressing   **+** =Making Advancements   **✓** =Shows Consistent Achievement

Child's Name	Physical Development																Notes
	P11	P12	P13	P14	P17	P18	P19	P20	P21	P22	P23	P24	P25	P26			
1.																	
2.																	
3.																	
4.																	
5.																	
6.																	
7.																	
8.																	
9.																	
10.																	
11.																	
12.																	
13.																	
14.																	
15.																	
16.																	
17.																	
18.																	
19.																	
20.																	

WINGS

WINGS Classroom Data Collection for Toddlers: 2 Year-Olds
SOCIAL/EMOTIONAL

Teacher _____ Classroom _____ Date _____

Stages of Progress: — =Regressing **+** =Making Advancements ✓=Shows Consistent Achievement

Child's Name	Social/Emotional							Notes
	SE12	SE13	SE14	SE15	SE16	SE17	SE18	
1.								
2.								
3.								
4.								
5.								
6.								
7.								
8.								
9.								
10.								
11.								
12.								
13.								
14.								
15.								
16.								
17.								
18.								
19.								
20.								

Classroom Data Collection for Toddlers: 2 Year-Olds
LANGUAGE & LITERACY

Teacher _____ Classroom _____ Date _____

Stages of Progress: — =Regressing **+** =Making Advancements ✓ =Shows Consistent Achievement

Child's Name	Language & Literacy																				Notes
	LL11	LL12	LL20	LL21	LL22	LL23	LL24	LL25	LL26	LL27	LL28	LL29	LL30								
1.																					
2.																					
3.																					
4.																					
5.																					
6.																					
7.																					
8.																					
9.																					
10.																					
11.																					
12.																					
13.																					
14.																					
15.																					
16.																					
17.																					
18.																					
19.																					
20.																					

Classroom Data Collection for Toddlers: 2 Year-Olds
WiNGS APPROACHES TO LEARNING

Teacher _____ Classroom _____ Date _____

Stages of Progress: — =Regressing   **+** =Making Advancements   ✓ =Shows Consistent Achievement

Child's Name	Language & Literacy					Notes
	AL10	AL11	AL12	AL13	AL14	
1.						
2.						
3.						
4.						
5.						
6.						
7.						
8.						
9.						
10.						
11.						
12.						
13.						
14.						
15.						
16.						
17.						
18.						
19.						
20.						

Classroom Data Collection for Toddlers: 2 Year-Olds
COGNITIVE

Teacher_____ Classroom_____ Date_____

Stages of Progress: — =Regressing   **+** =Making Advancements   ✓=Shows Consistent Achievement

Child's Name	Cognitive																	Notes
	C-M1	C-M2	C-M3	C-M4	C-M5	C-M6	C-M7	C-SI3	C-SI4	C-SS3	C-SS4	C-TP2	C-TP3	C-CD2	C-CD3	C-CD4	C-CD5	
1.																		
2.																		
3.																		
4.																		
5.																		
6.																		
7.																		
8.																		
9.																		
10.																		
11.																		
12.																		
13.																		
14.																		
15.																		
16.																		
17.																		
18.																		
19.																		
20.																		

Classroom Data Collection for Preschoolers: 3 Year-Olds
PHYSICAL DEVELOPMENT

Teacher_____ Classroom_____ Date_____

Stages of Progress: — =Regressing   + =Making Advancements   ✓ =Shows Consistent Achievement

Child's Name	Physical Development														Notes
	P12	P13	P14	P17	P18	P21	P22	P23	P24	P25	P26	P27	P28	P29	
1.															
2.															
3.															
4.															
5.															
6.															
7.															
8.															
9.															
10.															
11.															
12.															
13.															
14.															
15.															
16.															
17.															
18.															
19.															
20.															

Classroom Data Collection for Preschoolers: 3 Year-Olds
SOCIAL/EMOTIONAL

Teacher_____ Classroom_____ Date_____

Stages of Progress: **−** =Regressing   **+** =Making Advancements   ✓=Shows Consistent Achievement

Child's Name	Social/Emotional											Notes
	SE13	SE16	SE17	SE18	SE19	SE20	SE21	SE22	SE23		
1.											
2.											
3.											
4.											
5.											
6.											
7.											
8.											
9.											
10.											
11.											
12.											
13.											
14.											
15.											
16.											
17.											
18.											
19.											
20.											

WINGS Classroom Data Collection for Preschoolers: 3 Year-Olds
LANGUAGE & LITERACY

Teacher_____ Classroom_____ Date_____

Stages of Progress: — = Regressing   + = Making Advancements   ✓ = Shows Consistent Achievement

Child's Name	Language & Literacy														Notes
	LL11	LL12	LL21	LL23	LL24	LL29	LL30	LL31	LL32	LL33	LL34	LL35	LL36	LL37	LL38	
1.																
2.																
3.																
4.																
5.																
6.																
7.																
8.																
9.																
10.																
11.																
12.																
13.																
14.																
15.																
16.																
17.																
18.																
19.																
20.																

Classroom Data Collection for Preschoolers: 3 Year-Olds
APPROACHES TO LEARNING

Teacher_____ Classroom_____ Date_____

Stages of Progress: **−** =Regressing **+** =Making Advancements **✓** =Shows Consistent Achievement

Child's Name	Cognitive					Notes
	AL14	AL15	AL16	AL17	AL18	
1.						
2.						
3.						
4.						
5.						
6.						
7.						
8.						
9.						
10.						
11.						
12.						
13.						
14.						
15.						
16.						
17.						
18.						
19.						
20.						

WINGS

Classroom Data Collection for Preschoolers: 3 Year-Olds
COGNITIVE

Teacher _____ Classroom _____ Date _____

Stages of Progress: − =Regressing + =Making Advancements ✓ =Shows Consistent Achievement

Child's Name	Cognitive																			Notes
	C-M3	C-M6	C-M7	C-M8	C-M9	C-M10	C-M11	C-SI5	C-SI6	C-SI7	C-SI8	C-SS5	C-SS6	C-SS7	C-TP2	C-TP3	C-TP4	C-CD6	C-CD7	C-CD8	C-CD9
1.																					
2.																					
3.																					
4.																					
5.																					
6.																					
7.																					
8.																					
9.																					
10.																					
11.																					
12.																					
13.																					
14.																					
15.																					
16.																					
17.																					
18.																					
19.																					
20.																					

Classroom Data Collection for Preschoolers: 4-5 Year-Olds
PHYSICAL DEVELOPMENT

Teacher_____ Classroom_____ Date_____

Stages of Progress: **−** =Regressing   **+** =Making Advancements   **✓** =Shows Consistent Achievement

Child's Name	Physical Development																				Notes
	P12	P13	P14	P17	P18	P21	P22	P23	P24	P25	P26	P27	P28	P29	P30	P31					
1.																					
2.																					
3.																					
4.																					
5.																					
6.																					
7.																					
8.																					
9.																					
10.																					
11.																					
12.																					
13.																					
14.																					
15.																					
16.																					
17.																					
18.																					
19.																					
20.																					

WINGS Classroom Data Collection for Preschoolers: 4-5 Year-Olds
SOCIAL/EMOTIONAL

Teacher _____ Classroom _____ Date _____

Stages of Progress: — =*Regressing* **+** =*Making Advancements* ✓ =*Shows Consistent Achievement*

Child's Name	Social/Emotional											Notes
	SE13	SE16	SE17	SE18	SE19	SE20	SE21	SE22	SE23			
1.												
2.												
3.												
4.												
5.												
6.												
7.												
8.												
9.												
10.												
11.												
12.												
13.												
14.												
15.												
16.												
17.												
18.												
19.												
20.												

Classroom Data Collection for Preschoolers: 4-5 Year-Olds
LANGUAGE & LITERACY

Teacher_____ Classroom_____ Date_____

Stages of Progress: −=*Regressing*   +=*Making Advancements*   ✓=*Shows Consistent Achievement*

Child's Name	Language & Literacy																	NOTES
	LL11	LL12	LL21	LL23	LL32	LL33	LL35	LL36	LL39	LL40	LL41	LL42	LL43	LL44	LL45	LL46	LL47	LL48
1.																		
2.																		
3.																		
4.																		
5.																		
6.																		
7.																		
8.																		
9.																		
10.																		
11.																		
12.																		
13.																		
14.																		
15.																		
16.																		
17.																		
18.																		
19.																		
20.																		

WiNGS Classroom Data Collection for Preschoolers: 4-5 Year-Olds
APPROACHES TO LEARNING

Teacher _____ Classroom _____ Date _____

Stages of Progress: — =Regressing + =Making Advancements ✓ =Shows Consistent Achievement

Child's Name	Social/Emotional							Notes
	AL16	AL18	AL19	AL20	AL21	AL22	
1.							
2.							
3.							
4.							
5.							
6.							
7.							
8.							
9.							
10.							
11.							
12.							
13.							
14.							
15.							
16.							
17.							
18.							
19.							
20.							

Classroom Data Collection for Preschoolers: 4-5 Year-Olds
COGNITIVE

Teacher _____ Classroom _____ Date _____

Stages of Progress: **−** =Regressing **+** =Making Advancements **✓** =Shows Consistent Achievement

Child's Name	Cognitive																					
	C-M9	C-M12	C-M13	C-M14	C-M15	C-M16	C-SI5	C-SI9	C-SI10	C-SI11	C-SI12	C-SS5	C-SS6	C-SS8	C-SS9	C-SS10	C-TP2	C-TP3	C-TP4	C-CD6	C-CD7	C-CD8	C-CD9
1.																							
2.																							
3.																							
4.																							
5.																							
6.																							
7.																							
8.																							
9.																							
10.																							
11.																							
12.																							
13.																							
14.																							
15.																							
16.																							
17.																							
18.																							
19.																							
20.																							

My Ideal Daily Activity Schedule

Age Group _____

Time Period (Ex.: 7:00–7:15 a.m.)	Allotted Time (Ex.: 15 Minutes)	Activities (What will the children do?)

*During Exploration, children engage in self–selected activities.

Individualized Schedules:
▶ Each infant is fed according to his/her individual feeding plan.
▶ Diaper checks are performed every 2 hours and other times as needed.
▶ Each infant is allowed to sleep according to his/her individual sleeping pattern.

Personal Care Routines:
✓ Diaper checks are performed every 2 hours and other times as needed.
✓ Potty breaks are taken prior to each activity.
✓ Hand washing is performed upon arrival, before and after meals, after diapering/toileting, after outdoor play, after handling pets, after sensory play, after art activities, after sneezing, and other times as needed.
✓ Self–help skills are ongoing and are incorporated throughout the day.

WiNGS Daily Activity Form for Infants & 1 Year–Olds

Child's Name _____ Date _____

Arrival Time _____ Departure Time _____

Feedings

Amount Brought _____   Amount Remaining _____

Amount Used _____

Time	Amount	Initials	Time	Amount	Initials

Diapering   Diaper Codes (W=Wet; BM=Bowel Movement; D=Dry)

Diapers Brought _____   # Diapers Used _____   # Diapers Remaining _____

Time	Diaper	Initials	Time	Diaper	Initials

Sleeping

Time Down	Time Up	Initials	Time Down	Time Up	Initials

Comments:

WINGS Developmental Activity Plan for Infants

Week Of _____ Teacher(s) _____

Developmental Goals	Cognitive Activities	Physical Activities	Social-Emotional Activites	Language & Literacy Activites
Name: *Goals:*				
Name: *Goals:*				
Name: *Goals:*				
Name: *Goals:*				
Name: *Goals:*				
Name: *Goals:*				

Outdoor Exploration:

Teacher Tasks/Notes:

WINGS Weekly Plan for Infants: Exploration

Week Of _____ Teacher(s) _____ Theme _____

NATURE/SCIENCE	SOFT & COZY BOOK AREA	MUSIC & MOVEMENT

FINE MOTOR PLAY	DRAMATIC PLAY	GROSS MOTOR PLAY

Weekly Plan for Infants: Group Engagement

	MONDAY	TUESDAY	WEDNESDAY	THURSDAY	FRIDAY
Opening Activities					
Story Time					
Music & Movement					
Closing Activities					

Special Activities:

Special Needs:

45

WiNGS Weekly Plan for Toddlers: Exploration

Week Of _____ Teacher(s) _____ Theme/Studies _____

Key Concepts _____

TABLE TOYS	BLOCKS	CREATIVE ART
NATURE/SCIENCE	**SOFT & COZY BOOK AREA**	**MUSIC & MOVEMENT**
SENSORY PLAY	**DRAMATIC PLAY**	**GROSS MOTOR PLAY**

Outdoor Activities:

Special Needs: .... Special Activities: ....

Teacher Tasks/Notes:

WINGS Weekly Plan for Toddlers: Group Engagement

Week Of _____

	Monday	Tuesday	Wednesday	Thursday	Friday
Opening Activities					
Story Time					
Music & Movement					
Whole–Group Activities					
Closing Activities					

Small Group Activities Weekly Planning for Toddlers

(To be used with *WINGS Weekly Plan for Toddlers: Group Engagement*)

Week Of _____ Teacher(s) _____

Concepts	Activities
1.	1. Materials/Instructions:
2.	2. Materials/Instructions:
3.	3. Materials/Instructions:
4.	4. Materials/Instructions:

Group Assignments	
Groups	**Group Members**
A Group Name:	
B Group Name:	
C Group Name:	
D Group Name:	

WINGS Weekly Plan for Preschoolers/Pre–K: Exploration

Week Of _____ Teacher(s) _____ Theme/Studies _____

Key Concepts _____

MATH & MANIPULATIVES	BLOCKS & WOODWORKING	CREATIVE ART
NATURE/SCIENCE	**SOFT & COZY BOOK AREA**	**WRITING**
SENSORY PLAY	**DRAMATIC PLAY**	**MUSIC & MOVEMENT**

Outdoor Activities: ....

Curricular Links: ....

Community Connections:

WINGS Weekly Plan for Preschoolers/Pre–K: Group Engagement

Week Of _____ Teacher(s) _____ Theme/Studies _____

	Monday	Tuesday	Wednesday	Thursday	Friday
Opening Activities					
Small Groups 1. 2. 3. 4.	1. 2. 3. 4.	1. 2. 3. 4.	1. 2. 3. 4.	1. 2. 3. 4.	Child Choice Day
Story Time/Character Education *Character Word:*					
Music/Creative Movement					
Whole–Group Activities					
Closing Activities					

Special Needs: ....

Special Activities: ....

Teacher Tasks/Notes:

Small Group Activities Weekly Planning for Preschoolers/Pre-K

(To be used with *WINGS Weekly Plan for Preschoolers/Pre–K: Group Engagement*)

Week Of _____ Teacher(s) _____

Concepts	Activities
1.	1. Materials/Instructions:
2.	2. Materials/Instructions:
3.	3. Materials/Instructions:
4.	4. Materials/Instructions:

Group Assignments	
Groups	**Group Members**
A Group Name:	
B Group Name:	
C Group Name:	
D Group Name:	

WiNGS Weekly Plan for Blended Classrooms: Exploration

Week Of _____ Teacher(s) _____ Theme/Studies _____

Key Concepts _____

TABLE TOYS (Toddlers) / MATH & MANIPULATIVES (Preschoolers)	BLOCKS (Toddlers) / BLOCKS/WOODWORKING (Preschoolers)	WRITING (Preschoolers)
NATURE/SCIENCE	SOFT & COZY BOOK AREA	CREATIVE ART
SENSORY PLAY	DRAMATIC PLAY	MUSIC & MOVEMENT
GROSS MOTOR PLAY (Infants/Toddlers)	FINE MOTOR PLAY (Infants)	OUTDOOR PLAY

Special Needs:

Special Activities: Curricular Links:

Teacher Tasks/Notes: Community Connections:

WiNGS Weekly Plan for Blended Classrooms: Group Engagement

Week Of _____ Teacher(s) _____ Theme/Studies _____

	Monday	Tuesday	Wednesday	Thursday	Friday
Opening Activities					
Small Groups 1. 2. 3. 4.	1. 2. 3. 4.	1. 2. 3. 4.	1. 2. 3. 4.	1. 2. 3. 4.	Child Choice Day
Story Time/Character Education *Character Word:*					
Music/Creative Movement					
Whole–Group Activities					
Closing Activities					

Special Needs:

Special Activities: ....

Teacher Tasks/Notes: ....

Small Group Activities Weekly Planning for Blended Classrooms

(To be used with *WINGS Weekly Plan for Blended Classrooms: Group Engagement*)

Week Of _____ Teacher(s) _____

Concepts	Activities
1.	1. Materials/Instructions:
2.	2. Materials/Instructions:
3.	3. Materials/Instructions:
4.	4. Materials/Instructions:

Group Assignments

Groups	Group Members
A Group Name:	
B Group Name:	
C Group Name:	
D Group Name:	

WiNGS Weekly Plan for Family/Group Day Care: Exploration

Week Of _____ Teacher(s) _____ Theme/Studies _____

Key Concepts _____

TABLE TOYS (Toddlers) / MATH & MANIPULATIVES (Preschoolers)	BLOCKS (Toddlers) / BLOCKS/WOODWORKING (Preschoolers)	WRITING (Preschoolers)
NATURE/SCIENCE	SOFT & COZY BOOK AREA	CREATIVE ART
SENSORY PLAY	DRAMATIC PLAY	MUSIC & MOVEMENT
GROSS MOTOR PLAY (Infants/Toddlers)	FINE MOTOR PLAY (Infants)	OUTDOOR PLAY

Special Needs:

Special Activities: .... Curricular Links:

Teacher Tasks/Notes: .... Community Connections:

WINGS Weekly Lesson Plan for Family/Group Day Care

Provider _____   Week Of _____

Theme/Studies _____

Developmental Play/Group Engagement

Time	Activity
Opening–8:00	Arrivals, Health Check, Exploration*
8:00–9:00	Prep for Breakfast, Breakfast, Hand Washing, Cleanup
9:00–9:15	Opening Activity/Circle Time Mon: Tue: Wed: Thu: Fri:
9:15–10:15	Exploration* for Toddlers & Preschoolers, Developmental Play for Infants
10:15–10:45	Outdoor Play
10:45–11:15	Hand Washing, Exploration* for Infants, Small Group Activities. Alternate Small–Group Activity Time with Toddlers & Preschoolers (15 min.)

	Toddlers	Preschoolers
	Mon:	Mon:
	Tue:	Tue:
	Wed:	Wed:
	Thu:	Thu:
	Fri:	Fri:

Time	Activity
11:15–11:30	Cleanup, Music & Movement Mon: Tue: Wed: Thu: Fri:
11:30–12:30	Prep for Lunch, Lunch, Hand Washing, Cleanup

	12:30–12:45	Story Time/Character Education
		Mon:
		Tue:
		Wed:
		Thu:
		Fri:
	12:45–2:00	Quiet Time
	2:00–2:30	Outdoor Play
	2:30–2:45	Hand Washing, Music & Movement
		Mon:
		Tue:
		Wed:
		Thu:
		Fri:
	2:45–3:00	Closing Activity/Circle Time (Songs, Discussion, Review of Day)
		Mon:
		Tue:
		Wed:
		Thu:
		Fri:
	3:00–Closing	Extended Day Activities, Snack, Exploration*, Outdoor Play

*During Exploration, children engage in self–selected activities.

<u>Infants</u>: Gross & Fine Motor Play, Music & Movement, Dramatic Play, Soft & Cozy Book Area.

<u>Toddlers & Preschoolers</u>: Dramatic Play, Nature/Science, Creative Art, Sensory Play, Music & Movement, Table Toys/Manipulatives, Gross Motor Play, Soft & Cozy Book Area, and Block Play.

**Hand–washing is performed upon arrival, before and after meals, after diapering/toileting, after outdoor play, after handling pets, after sensory play, after art activities, after sneezing, and other times as needed.

Individualized Schedules:
- ▶ Each infant is fed according to his/her individual feeding plan.
- ▶ Each infant is allowed to sleep according to his/her individual sleeping pattern.
- ▶ Diaper/pull–up checks are performed every 2 hours and other times as needed.

Weekly Lesson Plan for Extended Day/After-School Care Programs: Infants

Provider _____   Week Of _____

Theme/Studies _____

Time	Activity
3:00–3:15	Story Time Mon: Tue: Wed: Thu: Fri:
3:15–4:00	Afternoon Snack
4:00–4:30	Outdoor Play
4:30–5:00	Music Activities Mon: Tue: Wed: Thu: Fri:
5:00–6:00	Exploration*/Developmental Play

*During Exploration, infants engage in self-selected activities—Soft & Cozy Book Area, Nature/Science, Music & Movement, Dramatic Play, Gross and Fine Motor Play.

Individualized Schedules:
- Each infant is fed according to his/her individual feeding plan.
- Diaper checks are performed every 2 hours and other times as needed.
- Each infant is allowed to sleep according to his/her individual sleeping pattern.

Weekly Lesson Plan for Extended Day/After-School Care Programs: Toddlers

Provider _____   Week Of _____

Theme/Studies _____

Time	Activity
3:00–3:30	**Whole Group Activities/Story Time** Mon: Tue: Wed: Thu: Fri:
3:30–4:00	Afternoon Snack
4:00–4:45	Exploration*
4:45–5:15	Outdoor Play
5:15–6:00	**Exploration*/Closing Activity** Mon: Tue: Wed: Thu: Fri:

*During Exploration, toddlers engage in self-selected activities—Dramatic Play, Nature/Science, Creative Art, Sensory Play, Music & Movement, Table Toys, Gross Motor Play, Soft & Cozy Book Area, and Block Play.

**Diaper/pull-up checks are performed every 2 hours and other times as needed.

Weekly Lesson Plan for Extended Day/After-School Care Programs: Preschoolers/Pre-K

Provider _____   Week Of _____

Theme/Studies _____

Time	Activity
3:00–3:30	**Whole Group Activities/Story Time** Mon: Tue: Wed: Thu: Fri:
3:30–4:00	Afternoon Snack
4:00–4:45	**Exploration*/Small Group Activities** Mon: Tue: Wed: Thu: Fri:
4:45–5:15	Outdoor Play
5:15–6:00	**Exploration*/Closing Activity** Mon: Tue: Wed: Thu: Fri:

*During Exploration, children engage in self-selected activities—Writing, Dramatic Play, Math & Manipulatives, Nature/Science, Creative Art, Sensory Play, Music & Movement, Soft & Cozy Book Area, and Blocks & Woodworking.

WINGS Daily Health Check Form

Children's Names	Pulse	Temperature	Speech	Skin (Scratches/Rash/Bruises)	Scalp	Chest	Neck	Throat	Face	Fingernails	Behavior	Extremities	General Appearance	Comments

WINGS Student Incident Report Form

Child's Name _____   Home Address _____

School _____   Class _____   Time of Incident _____

Date _____   Place of Incident _____

Nature of Incident _____

Description of how incident happened _____

_____

_____

Action Taken (Give specific details.) _____

_____

_____

Who observed the incident? _____

List name(s) of teacher(s) responsible for supervision of child _____

_____

Contacted Parent   ☐ Yes   ☐ No

Method of Contact   ☐ Phone   ☐ Note   ☐ Face-to-Face   ☐ Email

Teacher Making Report _____

Supervisor's Signature _____   Date _____

Parent(s) Signature _____   Date _____

Instructions: The original document of this report shall be placed in the program's files and one copy submitted to the Program Director on the day of the incident. The incident report includes any injury or accident that involves the child and should only be discussed with a parent or guardian of the child.

WINGS All About My Day/Week

Child's Name _____ Day/Week _____

W	**I**	**N**	**G**	**S**
Wonder	**I**nterests	**N**eeds	**G**oals	**S**kills
I am curious about:	I am interested in:	I am in need of:	I am learning to: Cognitive: Physical: Social/Emotional: Approaches to Learning: Language/Literacy:	I am taking steps by: Cognitive: Physical: Social/Emotional: Approaches to Learning: Language/Literacy:

Date Completed _____   Teacher(s) _____

WINGS Parent Orientation Checklist

Parent Orientation is scheduled for each family prior to the start of their child in the program. Program policies, procedures, and updates are provided annually during Open House, held prior to the start of each new school year.

The minimum listed items must be covered during orientation and/or classroom visitation.

- ❏ Arrival/Departure Procedures
- ❏ Absenteeism or Tardiness
- ❏ Inventory/Needs (Diapers, food, supplies, etc.)
- ❏ Overview of WINGS Curriculum
- ❏ Daily Classroom Schedule
- ❏ Feeding Methods (self, with help, etc.)
- ❏ Communication Procedures
    - ❏ Infant/Toddler Daily Activity Form
    - ❏ All About My Day/Week Form
    - ❏ Introduce Parent Cubbies
    - ❏ Parent Conferences
    - ❏ Assessment & Evaluation Forms
- ❏ Sanitation Procedures
    - ❏ Furniture and Toys (methods and frequency)
    - ❏ Emphasize Procedures for Children Who Are Ill or Who Become Ill
- ❏ Tour Classroom
- ❏ Invite Questions

WINGS Parent Conference Form

Date _____   Time _____

Child's Name _____   Teacher(s) _____

Names of Attendees

1.	4.
2.	5.
3.	6.

Topics Discussed

_____
_____
_____
_____

Recommendations

_____
_____
_____
_____

Comments

_____
_____
_____
_____

Signatures

I have reviewed the meeting minutes.

Parent(s) _____   Date _____

Teacher(s) _____   Date _____

WiNGS Parent Conference Evaluation

Date _____

1. How do you rate the conference overall?

   ☐ Excellent
   ☐ Good
   ☐ Fair
   ☐ Poor

2. How do you rate the way the teacher reported your child's progress?

   ☐ Excellent
   ☐ Good
   ☐ Fair
   ☐ Poor

3. If you could change anything about this conference, what would it be?

4. What other information would be helpful to you?

5. Do you have any additional comments?

WINGS Home Connections

Dear Parents,

In an effort to support your child's education, it is necessary for families to reinforce concepts we are learning at school in the home. Research illustrates that parent involvement overwhelmingly affects student success.

Please share activities you have done at home with your child this week to support the development of their cognitive, physical, social/emotional and language/literacy skills.

Child's Name: _____ Week of: _____

Developmental Domain	Home-learning Activities
Physical Large and small muscle development *Ex: Walking, scribbling*	M: T: W: R:
Social/Emotional Relationships and feelings *Ex: Positive interactions, encouragement*	M: T: W: R:
Language/Literacy Speaking, listening, reading, writing *Ex: Reading a book, having a discussion*	M: T: W: R:
Cognitive Mental processes, thinking skills *Ex: Counting, puzzle time, family games*	M: T: W: R:

Date Completed _____ Parent(s) _____

Notes

Notes

About the Author

Bisa Batten Lewis, Ed.D. ("Dr. Bisa") is a published author of education and parenting articles, college textbooks, children's books, early childhood curriculum, adult education curriculum, early learning handbooks, educational music for children and more. Having supervised multiple child development centers and college lab schools, facilitated programs from preschool to the university level, and provided adult curriculum and training to enhance the workforce, Dr. Bisa offers realistic methods of implementing quality research-based curriculum.

Professing as a life goal to advocate for children, Dr. Bisa is actively committed to upgrading the quality of early learning settings around the world. Her diverse experiences in early care and education have taught her the importance of providing practical curriculum and training materials that outline the most appropriate strategies for engaging children in learning.

Dr. Bisa earned Doctor of Education and Master of Education Degrees in Adult Education at the University of Georgia and Master of Education and Bachelor of Science Degrees in Early Childhood Education at Albany State University.